The Story Teller

An orphan's journey to enlightenment and freedom.

Joe Legolvan

Brian Laberge

Table of Contents

Prologue

"Everyone searches for Happiness but only a few realize Happiness is what they truly are."-The Storyteller

Walking through the cold steel computer-operated doors of the jail I saw all types of men, from murderers, gang members and drug addicts to the occasional DUI picked up the previous night after a few too many drinks at a corporate function. After nearly a decade as a spiritual counselor in the jail system, I saw many different faces every week, yet behind them there seemed to be a similar feeling that I had at times recalled in my own life. A feeling as deep and dark as a grave, where fear and depression seemed to be my only ally. A place where the stories are filled with anger, disappointment, anxieties, and regret. A place where destructive highs are a temporary relief from painful experiences and dark memories. Yet, even in the midst of this seemingly hopeless darkness I could feel the overwhelming comfort and joy that was shining beyond the cracks of even our darkest stories. It is this light that inspired this book.

In the jails I have seen firsthand the power and transformation that comes from learning a new story about who we are. These men were able to rebuild and reinvigorate their lives in profoundly impactful ways that altered their perceptions and experience. These kinds of changes can often take place in extreme and dire circumstances when people have nowhere else to turn. I have met some of the happiest and incredibly peaceful people behind bars, due to a suffering induced search within. Yet, these life changing self-realizations can at times be overlooked by comfortable lives that have not been strained to see beyond personal struggles.

Growing up in middle-class America, I did not see people without access to opportunities, adequate nutrition, or shelter. I did, however, see people who suffered from an internal dialogue based on a false perception that haunted their experience and hindered their potential and peace, keeping them living in a cycle of depression, anxiety and suffering. I saw beloved friends overdose on drugs in their struggle to numb pain. I saw a close family member who lived in a cycle of fear and depression take her own life when it became too hard to bear. I saw a society pathologized and become the mental patterns with which its people identified. Personally, I saw how, at times, I had accepted many negative beliefs about myself, which took away my peace, confidence, and sense of connection.

Fortunately, my life has been blessed with many great teachers who helped me see beyond these stories to the peaceful reality so easily forgotten. In the story about to unfold, the "blissful man" appropriately named Ananda (meaning "bliss" in Sanskrit) leads our main character Refugio through a multifaceted enlightenment. Although one man in the book, Ananda is a playful and joyful conglomeration of the many teachers that have helped me through some of my personal struggles. One of my favorite conversations with one of these teachers goes as follows:

Q: "Why am I so troubled by my mind and you seem to be free and happy and unaffected by yours?"

A: "The only difference between you and me is I know that the fear, suffering, and guilt my mind is producing is nonsense, while you believe deeply in yours. It is your belief in your chatter that is your bondage. It is simply my unbelief in my mind's chatter that is my freedom from it."

In other words, freedom from our personal stories of fear, loss, inadequacy, and other dark paths within our mind, is real liberation. Freedom does not require a confidence in our mind, but conversely, it requires the confidence that we are greater than our mind's creations.

I feel there are times in my life where I was able to relate to all of the different characters within the book. I have felt curious and excited, depressed and lost, successful but empty, and also at times full of joy, love, and purpose. Each character in this book attempts to represents a different side of our personalities and the blissful man Ananda is a representation of our own personal higher power who joyfully guides us out of our own illusions and sufferings.

"Refugio," the central figure in our story, is named after an inmate I met in the Denver jail system. After one of my classes in the jail pod, he approached me to share an amazing experience in which he was in a fatal car accident and was reportedly "clinically dead" before being brought back to life by emergency workers. During this incident, he claimed that he left his body and saw a "tunnel of light" that welcomed him into a place full of love and eternity. He stated that after this experience, *"I was no longer afraid of death because I knew there was truly no such thing. I knew now that death will be one of the happiest days of my life, but I am here now to complete a purpose."*

This was not the first time I had heard a story like this and I knew that what this man had was a classic Near-Death Experience (NDE). (An NDE refers to someone who clinically dies for a period of time and then returns to tell a story of what they experienced in the afterlife. These have been studied extensively by Dr.'s and Clinicians due to their prevalence, striking similarities between subjects, and the profound change in outlook that occurs following an NDE. Statistically, more than 15 million Americans alone have what is known as an NDE. These experiencers vary by many cultures, ages, and religions, yet they seem to recall a remarkably similar experience of the afterlife. As a cofounder of the Near-Death Experience Group of Denver, the last decade I have heard literally hundreds of these stories. I am always surprised by the variety of speakers at our groups. We have heard NDE stories from lawyers, construction workers, nurses, doctors, and many other varieties of people. One of my favorite quotes from these NDE's, which summarizes many experiences, is as follows:

"You are more loved than you can even imagine, the other side is filled with eternal peace, forgiveness, and laughter. Relax, eternal love is what awaits us when we leave our bodies. You are here now for a purpose, and when that is complete you will return to a place you never really left.

Life is like one big play and when our role here is finished we go back to our true home. On the other side The Light has a wonderful sense of humor. We would look at some of the silly things I took so seriously in my life, and we would just be laughing at them. Life down here is an illusion it's a game don't take it so seriously!"

This of course does not mean one should live recklessly or without sense. It is simply the recognition that no matter what happens in this life, everything is and always will be ok. Even though Refugio, was in jail and obviously going through some tough life experiences, he exuded a confidence rarely seen in people on the outside who had considerably more favorable circumstances. This inmate Refugio reminded me of the joy, purpose, and love that is naturally radiated when one knows their eternal story beyond their temporary circumstances.

Having an eternal confidence may seem to require faith or a spiritual experience like the one spoken of by Refugio or these Near Death Experiencers. However, an eternal perspective, when examined through the fundamental laws of reality, surprisingly validates the eternal nature of all existence. The first law of thermodynamics states two major things: first, energy is always conserved—in other words, energy can never be created nor destroyed; and second, everything can be broken down into energy. When we examine this statement, we can see that whatever we call ourselves, the physical body, the brain and every other material object within our world is made up of energy, which can never be created nor destroyed, only transformed. The physical body is always changing and transforming and yet, energy eternally remains. To say it a different way, in this life we are constantly transforming, yet scientifically there was never a time, nor will there be a time in the future, where the fundamental substance of what we truly are will cease to exist.

Beyond sheer science there is a gut intuition that most humans possess that seems to point to something greater than just this temporary life. As a wise man once said, "Eternity is written in the hearts of all men." I hold a conviction that knowing the eternal nature of our life can change any story from a tale of darkness, suffering, and fear into one of joy, love and security. As my co-author, and quite possibly the happiest person I have ever met, Brian Laberge, once said, "Everyone is writing their own story, why not write a happy one that comes from our real self?"

An increasingly popular form of psychology, which has been shown to be useful in helping people navigate through mental struggles, is a practice called "cognitive therapy." In this method, a person tells his or her story from a different perspective, based on different beliefs, values, and self-image. It is this change in their perception and story which helps them see their life and situation in a less depressing form. In the story about to begin, our main character learns that he has the power to interpret his experiences through the eyes of his eternal self, regardless of how others, or his believed self, may see his life. Refugio is liberated from fears and insecurities that previously afflicted his life and begins living from a place of acceptance, love, and eternity. Our hope for this book is that it will do the same for all who read its words, and that they will be led to personally investigate and validate the concepts within their own life experience.

The title of this book is "The Storyteller," as a reminder of the power we all have to tell a different story. Many great teachers have taught the importance of choosing a positive story, but without a deep examination of our fundamental reality this positive thinking can seem naïve and baseless. It is for this reason that we attempt to reveal the logical explanation of why a positive outlook is the basis of our reality. Many of the ideas within do not require blind belief. On the contrary, the peaceful, comforting, and joy-filled perspective that evolves along our main character's journey should be the rational outcome of the examination of our world, personal experiences, and self.

The teachings in this book can be found in most religions yet do not belong to any religion, as it focuses on the metaphorical "picture" of these teachings and not the different styles of "frames." As this story continues to develop, our desire is to remind us of our identity as the eternal storyteller, trust our personal Higher Power, and to pleasantly inspire us to deeply experience the joy of this life.

In loving memory of Julia Legolvan and Lou Laberge

∞

When a wave crashes, you could consider this an ending or
a death, but ultimately it continues existing as the ocean.
The distinctions of time, life, and death only happen when
we define the wave as being separate from the ocean.

-THE STORYTELLER

The Storyteller

Chapter 1
Refugio's Story

All stories have a beginning and an ending, and this story begins and ends with a boy named Refugio (pronounced Raph-HUGE-ee-oh). The day was gloomy and wet, as if the weather took note of the melancholy occasion. Refugio embraced his orphan brothers and sisters' and said goodbye, with mutual tears in the eyes of his long-time companions. He had recently turned 18 years old, and because he had never been adopted, this was the day when he would finally be released from the orphanage.

The youngest ones cried the hardest, for they had looked up to Refugio for much needed comfort and care. He was treasured by his siblings in the orphanage for he carried a gentle and kind nature that made others feel loved and relaxed in his presence. Over the last few years he had become like a father figure. Now, in the difficult process of leaving his only known home, both he and his long-time companions grieved deeply.

Refugio lived in a world much like your own but he had an unusual ability that is not common to this world or your own. Before we get into Refugio's unique ability, let's explain a little bit about who he was, or at least who he thought he was. Refugio was namelessly dropped off at the local church when he was an infant. Never knowing who his parents were or where he came from, he lived his life with no idea who he really was.

Refugio had a fairly petite frame and looked quite young for his age. Exchanging goodbyes, he was smaller than many with whom he shared hugs. He had short brown hair, with penetrating dark features, and a large smile that thoroughly expressed his character. He dressed simply with whatever clothes were provided to him through the orphanage and didn't spend much time thinking about his appearance. Despite his simple dress and small stature, his presence was large, uplifting, and well respected.

Refugio lived the life of an ordinary boy who loved to play games, read books, and make new friends; however, he did have one unusual ability that set him apart from everyone he had ever met in his life. You see, Refugio had the extraordinary ability to know exactly what others were thinking and feeling simply by observing them. He would know people's names before they would introduce themselves. He saw and felt what people had on their minds at any moment. Sometimes he knew what they were planning to do in the future, or what they had done in their past. Whatever was on their minds at that moment, he could see as clearly as you are reading this book right now.

Because of this ability, Refugio's favorite activity was going to a local park to sit on a bench, where he spent hours watching the passing people's thoughts and emotions. He could hear all kinds of stories as many people traveled by him. Stories of excitement, stories of pain, stories of relationships, and stories of desire. Refugio watched these stories of all kinds as he enjoyed his own simple life, which he felt was fairly uneventful in comparison.

When there was no one else to observe, Refugio would appreciate the nature in the park. He watched the birds sing and play, and the plants and trees blow subtly in the wind, and he relished the clouds as they would form pictures in the sky. With this amazing dance of life and nature, Refugio was surprised to see that when he observed people, they were too focused on their own thoughts and emotions to enjoy, or hardly even see, the park. He smiled to himself while he continued to appreciate the glorious show of life cascading through his senses and enriching his enjoyment of the world. Experiencing deeply the fullness of this nature, he wondered: What could keep these people so occupied that they would miss out on all this beauty?

After Refugio had said his last goodbyes, he decided that, without having any other plan, he would do what he loved the most in life: go to the park and observe the people and their thoughts. However, on this day Refugio felt different. Refugio knew that today he could no longer call himself an orphan. He knew that now he was "grown up," and pondered what that really meant. He continued watching and sitting as usual, but the question became increasingly haunting. He saw so many others who seemed to know exactly who they were and what they were supposed to be doing. They had a past full of experiences, a future with expectations, fears, and hopes. They had families whom they loved, and dramas in their relationships. They had a place to call their home, and a community to which they belonged.

Suddenly, an unfamiliar feeling of insecurity hit Refugio as he began to wonder why he didn't have something like this in his life. He began to envy these people who had a great ongoing story that kept them occupied and, to Refugio, made them very important. Refugio sat and pondered this question and these new feelings that arose in his thoughts. "Who am I, and why don't I have a story?" This thought entered his mind and traveled deep into his heart, leaving him with a feeling of loss and emptiness.

Abruptly the wind picked up and Refugio could hear a faint laughing somewhere in the park. As he looked around to see if someone was near, an idea suddenly came upon Refugio. It hit Refugio with such force, it temporarily silenced all the other questions and feelings of insecurity that had arisen. He sat up with a sense of adventure and exhilaration and said out loud, "I will set out on a journey to find my own story!"

A few exciting moments passed when Refugio thought, "Where would someone go to find out who they are? I imagine it must be a long journey." He thought of the furthest place he had ever heard of, a place called The Dark Sea. He had seen a picture of this stunning place years ago in the orphanage, and it had inspired him with its dark waves and black sand that seemed to be never ending.

"This will be the perfect place to go to find out who I am! This is where I will find my own story!" Refugio said to himself as a contented smile lifted his face. Having made up his mind, a deep calm washed over him. He felt free from the insecurity, the questions, and the emptiness that had abruptly troubled him. Sitting back, he began to again enjoy the scenery. "Tomorrow," he said, "I will start on my journey, and discover my story."

∞

"Suddenly, his face in the reflection spoke: "Wake up!"
Startled, Refugio's eyes immediately opened and the
dreams disappeared into the morning sunrise and chirping
birds."

Chapter 2
The Vision

That night, Refugio slept under a large blue wish tree that had long branches full of dark blue leaves with light purple tips resembling feathers. As he began to doze off, he thought about what kind of a story he might have. When he finally fell asleep, he was welcomed by three dreams. In the first dream he was a powerful businessman. He felt proud as he enjoyed this dream of power and prestige but this experience left Refugio with a deep feeling of unexplainable discontent. Later, he dreamt he was a father and a husband. His heart warmed as he contemplated the love of his beautiful family. Yet, as the dream continued his love was overpowered by a fear of losing them. Finally, he dreamt he was a traveling sage who had endless wisdom to share. In this third and final dream, he walked past a river and noticed that his reflection, in the smooth flowing water, was that of a smiling face of an old man. Suddenly, his face in the reflection spoke: "Wake up!" Startled, Refugio's eyes immediately opened and the dreams disappeared into the morning sunrise and chirping birds.

He laid there a few minutes watching the morning scene and reflecting on his dreams. After a few moments of happily reminiscing about his remarkable night, he reminded himself that he was just plain Refugio, still without a story of his own. With a deep sigh, he got up and gathered his things, which included a backpack holding his blanket, a few pairs of clothes, a little money the orphanage had given him, and a canteen. As he stretched his body, he remembered his goal. Then he eagerly set off on his journey towards the Dark Sea to find his story.

∞

"He knew now without a doubt that finding out who he is would be the most important thing he could accomplish, and that no other distraction would keep him from his goal."

Chapter 3
Boss

Refugio had been on his journey for several hours when he finally left the familiar town of his orphanage and entered a place that looked to him to be very prosperous. All the buildings were new, the grass was freshly cut, the trees were trimmed, and the people he saw appeared to be dressed up. Feeling hungry and a little tired, Refugio promptly found a place to rest and eat. When he took a seat in the nicest restaurant Refugio had ever been in and looked over the menu, he was a little taken aback by the prices of food. Not wanting to embarrass himself by leaving, he decided to buy something small that he thought looked good but, most importantly, he could afford. While he was ordering, he heard a man say loudly, "The deal is done!" Refugio looked up and at once made eye contact with a boisterous, smiling man who was finishing what looked to be one of several moon dust drinks. (Moon Dust: a strong intoxicant that was popular among those who were looking to celebrate or relax).

Refugio could see that the man was excited and full of thoughts of money and success. The server taking Refugio's order acknowledged the boisterous man and said to him "I'll get the usual for you Boss." Staring at the man who was only a few feet away, Refugio was startled to see the man notice him.

"I don't recognize you, boy," he said to Refugio. "Are you from this town?" Refugio could instantly smell the man's breath, which was producing a strong strange odor from his multiple drinks.

"No, sir, I am not. I walked here today." Refugio admitted in a meek tone.

"Well, just so you know, you walked into MY town. Do you know who I am?"

"No, sir, I don't,"

"Well, young man, I am the wealthiest man in this town, and I own most of the businesses here. After the deal I just made today, I will have own more than ever. Today is a great day and a time for celebration! Let me buy your meal, Mr.…."

"Refugio is my name."

"Refugee what? That's a hard one. How about I call you R for short. I call everyone around here by nicknames. The waitress who took your order I call 'Dust' because she makes me the best moon dust in town. I call my driver 'Speed' because he can get me anywhere in no time. Until I find out what your talent is, I'll call you R!"

"Okay," Refugio said gracefully, though he felt slightly offended.

The man looked Refugio over.

"You don't look like you belong in this town, R. I'll bet you don't have a dime to your name, do you?"

Refugio was surprised by the question, but acknowledging the man's accurate observation on his financial situation, he shook his head yes.

"You remind me of myself when I was younger," the man said as he again studied Refugio. "Don't worry, young man, I will tell you a story about myself."

The man straightened his already straight tie and made a confident face that seemed to resemble a hero who had just saved the day.

"You see, R, I started out just like you, without anything or anyone to help me. Broke and a nobody, I worked my way up in a large company until I saved enough money to start my own. Now, 20 years later, I own nine businesses in which I am the boss over many people. I am respected by many around here in this town. Most people call me Boss."

"That's amazing!" said Refugio.

"Dust! Give this young man a drink." The man demanded.

A mug was slid to Refugio almost instantaneously, and it fizzed and foamed from the top of the glass.

"Take a drink, young man."

Refugio took a sip and was surprised by the instant euphoria. For a split moment, all of his thoughts left him: the journey, his purpose, and his incessant search for his story. Refugio felt, for the first time since he left on his journey, he had room to breathe from his mind's overbearing dialog. After a few seconds passed, so did the euphoria, leaving Refugio wanting another sip of moon dust.

The man was now even more closely inspecting Refugio. After a few awkward moments, he spoke.

"R, you caught me on a great day, and I am feeling generous. I will give you a job in one of my companies. Of course, it will be an entry position, but if you stick around I can show you how to become a wealthy man like myself. You are young and have a lot of life ahead of you. This is a great town with many opportunities, and you could make yourself an important person here, just like I did."

This was the most powerful man Refugio had ever met, and he was surprised at his fortune to meet the most powerful man in this beautiful town. He felt grateful for the boss's generous offer, and he certainly could use some money. He wondered for a moment of what it might feel like if he could have a story of being a powerful rich man. While he was listening to Boss speak, he began looking deeply into his thoughts, Refugio saw how this man was respected by others, owned many beautiful things, and had a great sense of importance within his mind and in the minds of others.

However, to Refugio's astonishment, as he looked closer there also appeared to be an emptiness and a sense of anxiety within this man's thoughts. In the back of Boss's mind was a continuous stream of worries that said, "Who would I be without all of this power and wealth? I must never lose any of it! I am nothing without my position? I must have more, more, more!" Refugio could also see that these thoughts were so haunting to this man that relief only came when he was intoxicated, which slowed his thinking process and temporarily calmed his deepest fears.

Refugio was astounded. This man seemed like he knew exactly who he was, and yet he was suffering from the same insecurity Refugio had. To Refugio's surprise, "Boss," with all his prestige, respect, and wealth still didn't know who he was. Beyond these loud thoughts which drove the majority of Boss's life, there was also a deeper and gloomier thought that seemed to be endlessly permeating the background saying, "What is the point of everything? What is the purpose of all this? Why am I here?"

A vacant and distant look came over Refugio's eyes and a long pause ensued. Boss tried to get Refugio's attention. "Hey, R. Hey, R!" he said loudly.

In a moment of clarity, Refugio stood up, loudly knocking his spoon on the ground. Everyone in the restaurant looked in his direction. Slightly startled by the immediate attention, Refugio paused before gathering up his courage.

"I must find out who I am!" he said confidently.

The man was confused, and now a little worried about R's mental state.

"Whatever you say, R," he said with a shrug of his shoulders. "Good luck with that. I'm going to celebrate this new deal. I'll see you around."

The room returned to its normal atmosphere as if nothing had happened, but in Refugio's mind he knew that something significant had just occurred. He knew now without a doubt that finding out who he is would be the most important thing he could accomplish, and that no other distraction would keep him from his goal.

Refugio thanked Dust for an amazing meal. He grabbed a few leftovers, including a delicious stuffed roll and some sort of fruit pudding that was one of the best things Refugio ever tasted, and put them in his backpack. With a stronger resolve, he continued on his journey.

∞

"As Refugio walked on, the man and the remains of the house completely disappeared in the distance; but the story this man had told Refugio about his life remained with him, like a dark cloud that followed his every step."

Chapter 4
Ashes of Sadness

As Refugio kept walking, he left the prosperous town and entered a beautiful countryside he had never seen before. He thought long and hard about Boss. He reflected on his thoughts about having a great story and what that really meant. Did adding things to himself, like prestige, power, and money, really make him better or worse? He didn't think money, power, or prestige was somehow a bad thing, but he now understood that it wouldn't answer the question that continued to plague his mind: "Who am I?"

The countryside was mostly barren except for a few houses separated by acres of sugarcane. Large clouds were moving in the same direction as Refugio, and with a playful excitement he began pretending that he was in a race with them. Running through fields, jumping over rocks and tree branches, he continued to outrun his unaware opponent above. The birds scattered in all directions as he raced through the landscape creating a commotion. Seeing a large branch ahead, he attempted an ambitious leap over it. Underestimating the size of the tree branch and overestimating his jumping ability, his foot caught the edge, causing him to flop into a large bush. Covered in leaves, he checked his body for injuries. After a full-body inspection to make sure he had not seriously hurt himself, he began laughing out loud. He laughed at his fall and failed jumping attempt, but he also laughed with a feeling of joy and adventure from his journey. With a smile and sense of gratitude, he picked up his scattered items, ensured that nobody was watching, brushed off the leaves, and continued on his way.

An hour later, he passed the remains of a large house that looked as if it had burnt down years ago. There was a large pile of ash and weathered caution signs surrounding a burn site. Ignoring the signs, Refugio began to explore the rubble. He saw the remains of scorched picture frames and other household items, almost unrecognizable from what looked to be a devastating fire that had never been cleaned up. Thinking he was the only person in the scorched remains, he was surprised when he heard the faint sound of crying. He walked towards the sound that was coming from behind a large rock chimney. Behind the chimney there was a man sitting in a pile of ash weeping to himself. Unaware of Refugio's presence, the man continued to sob. As Refugio began watching the man's thoughts, he saw a flood of depression and grief. The thoughts proclaimed: "My life is pointless. I lost everything I love. I was a horrible father! I should of, I could of…"

Refugio approached cautiously, and when the man saw that he was not alone he stopped crying.

"Sir, what is wrong?" Refugio asked gently.

The man, giving up on trying to hold back his tears, continued wailing.

"Everything I loved is gone," he said between gasps. "I had a house, a great family, and I lost everything." Refugio sensed that this man's anger and grief had been with him for years since the fire.

"I'm very sorry. Can I help you?" Refugio asked, feeling a sense of reverence for this man's great loss.

"Help me?" The man's sadness turned into an annoyed shout. "How can you help me? All that I had is gone! Do you know what that's like?! Do you?" Before Refugio could answer he shouted. "I should of, I could of!" The man said the last sentence out loud this time and Refugio wondered what it meant. Ignoring the man's last statement Refugio answered.

"I'm sorry, I don't know what that is like." He felt slightly frightened by the man's accusatory question.

"Ya, I bet you don't. I bet you have a large house and a family you love." The man said in a cynical tone.

"Well, not exactly, sir." Meekly replied Refugio. "You see, I have never had a family or a home that I could lose. I am an orphan."

The man's expression changed from a look of anger to one of pity.

"You never had a family or a home?" the man said, looking intensely at Refugio with bloodshot, tear-soaked eyes. "That is very sad. Having a family and a home is the best thing I had ever experienced. I am sorry that you never knew this joy."

The man and Refugio sat in silence for a moment while the man reflected deeply into Refugio's life. Refugio listened to the man's thoughts: "This boy is alone in life and actually has a story much worse than my own. This pitiful story is even worse than mine..."

The man's crying stopped. He stood up, grabbed a partially burnt picture frame, dusted off the ash, and with a look of sadness but also a sense of sympathy said to Refugio, "Good luck to you, boy."

The man continued rummaging through the burnt memorabilia. Refugio didn't say a word as he began slowly walking out of the ashes as if in a trance, deeply contemplating the man's words and thoughts. As Refugio walked on, the man and the remains of the house completely disappeared in the distance; but the story this man had told Refugio about his life remained with him, like a dark cloud that followed his every step.

∞

"Feeling deeply the story he now knew was his own, a cloud of depression seemed to transform the world around him."

Chapter 5
The Cloud of Depression

Refugio had set out on this journey to find out who he was, but now he began to regret his decision. He thought he would be something great, but he never knew how sad his real story was. "It would have been better if I never knew," he thought to himself. Hearing the echoes of the words the man had spoken to him in pity, Refugio realized that being an orphan without a home or family was itself a story. A sad story. Feeling deeply the story he now knew was his own, a cloud of depression seemed to transform the world around him.

He continued to walk in desperation, trying to remember the world he once knew, but everything somehow looked darker and gloomier than before. As he continued, he began to realize the nature that used to bring him joy now seemed separate and frightening to him. The trees appeared barren and dark, the moons and planets looked looming and conspiring, and the clouds seemed to overtake the sky to hide the stars. Refugio fell against a dead, dried up tree. Feeling the weight of hopelessness on his heart, he sat pondering who he now knew he was.

∞

"Even though you believe this limited sad story, realize that this story is your own. This restrictive, self-created story could never encompass the unlimited storyteller that you are."

Chapter 6
The Blissful Man

Clouded by grief, Refugio hardly noticed a man walking towards him. Out of the corner of his eye he saw a small figure approaching and eventually come to a stop a few feet away. Looking in the direction of the figure, Refugio saw a very kind looking fellow, with a great smile that stretched all the way to his twinkling eyes. He was short in stature with a small frame, like Refugio's, but he had long arms that now rested confidently on a cane directly in the center of his petite physique. The remaining hairs on his head were grey, untamed, and going in different directions.

Refugio and the man made eye contact, and then the man lifted his cane, directing Refugio to look at a tree a few feet in front of him. As he did so, Refugio was surprised to see a rare silk rainbow tree covered in blooming flowers of many different colors. This was the first silk rainbow tree Refugio had ever seen in real life and it looked more amazing than he had ever imagined. Gazing at this tree in awe, he suddenly felt a slight contentment and peace, temporarily forgetting the dark thoughts that had been haunting him. Sensing that Refugio was now conscious of his surroundings, and momentarily free from his thoughts, the man spoke in a gentle voice.

"Refugio is what you are called in this life," he said.

Refugio stood in silence, for he was not aware of anyone else who could also read minds, or who could pronounce his name correctly without his dictation. Refugio tried to read the man's mind to find out his name, but for some reason he could not. His mind was still overwhelmed by his own sad story, and it seemed to conceal his mind-reading abilities.

"What is your name?" asked Refugio, still feeling a bit dumbfounded.

"Ananda is what I am called in this world." The old man seemed to chuckle in a playful way after each word he spoke.

Refugio was still a little nervous meeting someone else who could read minds, so he stood still, unsure of what to say next. Sensing Refugio's nervousness, the man flashed an unassuming, playful grin and shook his head, as if to urge Refugio to ask more questions.

"If you know my name, you must also know my sad story," Refugio said, feeling calmed by this man's demeanor.

The smiling man lifted his arms in an animated expression, which caused the cane he was holding to hit a rock, creating a loud noise that shook Refugio.

"Refugio! Are you still dreaming or are you awake?" Ananda's voice had a stern yet gentle, almost humorous tone.

Refugio did not know what the man meant, and was at first thrown off completely by the question. Then, a flashback appeared in Refugio's mind of the dream he had the previous day. That old sage he had seen in the mirror's reflection in the dream—looked just like this man! Spurred by this realization, Refugio bent down and picked up the man's cane. As he lifted it into the light, he noticed that this cane had carvings of different trees that ran all the way up to the handle. He recognized a few of the trees, but there were others he had never seen before. After looking at the cane, he handed it to Ananda. He felt puzzled at meeting this man who looked so similar to the man in his dream, but also by his words. Ananda accepted back his cane with a smile and returned to his previous position of resting his arms on its handle.

"What do you mean, am I dreaming?" Refugio paused, reflecting on the man's words. "You actually look like someone I saw in my dream. Was that you?"

The man chuckled. "You tell me, Refugio, it was your dream," he said, and then he broke into a full laughter that was so pleasant, Refugio couldn't help but smile along with him, even though he was still thoroughly confused. Ananda calmed his laughter, though he still appeared to be holding back a grin.

"Refugio, I know you can also read minds," he said.

"I can," Refugio said confidently. He paused, thinking about his most recent experience trying to read Ananda's mind. "At least I could…I am having a difficult time now for some reason."

"That reason is the same reason most people cannot read minds. You now think you know who you are. You have accepted a story as your identity."

"A story as my identity?" thought Refugio.

"Yes, Refugio, you now believe you have a sad story, and you have accepted this story as who you are. Before you started on this journey you hadn't accepted a story yet. Your mind was not clouded by this sad story, and this gave you the freedom to see what others were thinking."

Ananda paused and looked at Refugio with a sincere expression. "Would you like to know who you really are?" he asked.

"You mean you can tell me my story?!" Refugio blurted out.

"Not exactly," Ananda paused and smiled. "Only you can do that. But I can show you something even better. I can remind you of who you are beyond all of your stories. The you that you have always been, with or without a story.

Refugio pondered this last statement slightly confused.

"I say remind you because deep down you already know. I am no different than you, Refugio, except I have remembered." Ananda's humble attitude was projected in his unassuming and gentle voice.

"Who I've always been?" replied Refugio with an expression of disbelief. "I have always been an orphan who never had a family. I don't mean to burst your bubble."

"Ha-ha!" Ananda laughed. "Don't worry about bursting my bubble. It is only when it pops that one can return to the state of being water."

Refugio was still confused by the man's metaphors. Ananda continued in a more serious and compassionate tone.

"You do have a unique personal experience of life as an orphan, but the sadness you have is not uncommon; it stems from a story of missing out on something you believe the rest of the world possesses. Even though you believe this limited sad story, realize that this story is your own. This restrictive, self-created story could never encompass the unlimited storyteller that you are."

∞

"I have come to remind you who you are, beyond what you think you are. You, Refugio, are more powerful and amazing than you have comprehended in your stories."

Chapter 7
The Storyteller

Refugio stood in silence, soaking in all that Ananda had been telling him. But his mind was still reeling with questions.

"What do you mean, sir, by storyteller?"

"You have heard many stories, but did you ever consider the one who is telling your story?" Ananda asked in an excited tone.

"Telling my story? I always thought it was my experiences that were telling me my story."

Ananda nodded. "Yes, you are experiencing through your body's senses, but these senses of yours are without any opinion. It is you, the storyteller, who decides what those experiences mean. You have heard many stories and some were given to you by other storytellers, but it is only you who has chosen to accept them as your own." Ananda laughed when he said this, as if he was delivering a punchline to the nature that surrounded them. Yet, Ananda's meek and gentle delivery made Refugio feel like he was laughing with him and not at him.

Ananda's conviction was startling to Refugio, and he was swimming in a sea of concepts he had never considered. It felt strange that this old man whom he had just met seemed to know so much about him. He wondered how they had so quickly entered into such a deep conversation, but something familiar about the man's presence gave Refugio comfort and an almost instant rapport with Ananda. Refugio was also still a little intimidated by Ananda's ability to read his mind, but his kind and almost comedic nature inspired Refugio to ask more questions.

"So you can tell me who I am?" he asked.

"Tell you who you are, or who you think you are?" Ananda quipped. "Actually, I can tell you both; but why don't you listen to my mind and see if I know who I am?"

Once more, Refugio was puzzled, but again he felt enamored with Ananda's expressive, playful demeanor. He concentrated deeply and after a few minutes, and with Ananda's peaceful presence to help, he was able to tune out all other thoughts and stories and look deeply into Ananda's mind.

To Refugio's amazement, Ananda's mind was still, in a great and profound silence that held a deep sense of confidence. This confidence seemed new to Refugio, but he remembered experiencing the same silence within himself. It was a silence of being free from a story, but it was unlike his mind because it was permeating with a fulfilling peace and joy, which in itself seemed to be telling a happy story. When he was reading the man's mind, the deep emotional highs that were experienced by Refugio reminded him of being a young child. Even though Ananda did not have a distracting, all-encompassing story, Refugio sensed that this blissful man truly knew who he was.

Refugio was the first to break the long silence.

"Your mind was filled with a sense of happiness I have never seen in anyone I have ever read. It was like you are silent and empty, yet full and fulfilled all at the same time."

Ananda looked intently at Refugio for a moment.

"I am neither empty or full because these are attributes of the mind, and I am beyond the states of the mind," he replied. "However, it is because of this silence in my mind that I can recognize who I truly am, beyond the stories of this world. The water must be still for one to properly see his own reflection."

"Beyond the mind and all the stories of the world?" Refugio said to himself. He had never thought of such an idea. He thought to himself, "What could be beyond all the stories of the world?"

"Refugio, the chattering you hear when you listen to others comes from a limited story that they believe themselves to be. I heard your chattering when I approached you. It was a sad story of loss, and if you would have let it endure, it would have continued to fill your mind with endless depressing thoughts. I have come to remind you who you are, beyond what you think you are. You, Refugio, are more powerful and amazing than you have comprehended in your stories."

∞

"Your emotions are not lying, and neither are your thoughts because whatever you believe will become true within YOUR experience. But YOUR truth, which is depressing, does not affect THE truth, which is blissful."

Chapter 8
Holding on to Sadness

Refugio had heard what Ananda said about stories and about who he was, but he felt he had to respond honestly.

"Beyond what I think I am?" he said. "You see, sir, I truly was an orphan, and never even had a family to enjoy or experience any love from. I felt deep sadness when I found out that I was missing something from my life. I know you may not understand my feelings, but this emotion is very real to me. Are you saying that my emotions and feelings are lying to me?"

"No, Refugio, your emotions are not lying, and neither are your thoughts because whatever you believe will become true within YOUR experience. But YOUR truth, which is depressing, does not affect THE truth, which is blissful." Ananda meekly giggled but returned to his sincere tone. "When deep emotion is felt with any story, one will believe that story deeper than any other, but this does not make this story any more real than any other. I am not denying that your emotions and thoughts are real to you, but I am saying that you are the storyteller that is interpreting both of them. At every moment you are creating the

49

interpretation of your life. Whatever you interpret you will experience as YOUR story, and that will become YOUR interpretation of your truth."

Ananda's words seemed to transfer pictures that appeared in Refugio's mind, and those pictures explained more than the words could convey. He stared deeply into the plants in front of him as he listened, but his attention was on more interesting images within his mind.

"You not only create this interpretation of experiences when you are awake, but also when you go to sleep and dream," Ananda continued. "During your dreams you temporarily forget your 'awake' story and create a new 'dream' one. Sometimes you dream an amazing and happy dream, which you may not want to wake up from. Other times your dreams are so sad and frightening that you are relieved to wake up. The truth is you are waking up from a sleeping dream into a waking dream. Many are dreaming their lives away, never awakening to the blissful reality that life truly is."

Refugio felt a little irritation that Ananda had barely acknowledged his past, but he also felt a little better, no longer mired in the darkness of his thoughts haunting him. As if the sky was responding to his new mental state, the clouds began to dissipate above both Ananda and Refugio, revealing a beautiful canvas of galaxies, planets, and moons. Refugio looked at the sky, then glanced down at Ananda.

"So you're telling me that my past is only a story. That isn't real?" Refugio asked.

Ananda looked compassionately at Refugio.

"Refugio, I'm not saying your past experiences were not real, but the story about those PAST experiences is being told PRESENTLY by you. Whatever story you are telling yourself about your past experiences can change any time you give up your belief in them. In your case, you believed what another storyteller said to you about your own past experiences. I am not telling you what to believe about your experiences, just simply that you are the one who is deciding what to believe."

Ananda was slowly pacing and observing the nature around him while he spoke, touching the leaves of the plants and putting his hand on tree trunks. He seemed to be communicating with the plants, like a gardener tending lovingly to his garden.

∞

"Sometimes when people hear a story told by another storyteller, they give away their freedom and believe whatever that story is," Ananda noted. "People can exist in these stories for entire lifetimes. It can be difficult to let go of these stories because they are sometimes told to them by people that they respect and love. But really, it doesn't matter who it came from. All that matters is if you STILL believe the story."

Chapter 9
How do I Know

Refugio was interested in these ideas but far from convinced. He sat there thinking for a few minutes and then, with an inquisitive defiance, he said, "These are all interesting concepts, but how do I know that what you are saying is true?"

"Yes, Refugio, how do you know that anything is true? Only by your own experience. You can hear about a recipe for an apple pie, but it will not give you the experience of tasting one. Similarly, these concepts will not give you the experience of truth. They must be experienced for yourself. However, having a recipe to make a pie can help you save much time and disappointment from the trial and error of not using the proper ingredients."

These images prompted a smile and slight hunger from Refugio. Refugio began rummaging through his bag as Ananda talked, looking for his leftover food.

"Having an intellectual understanding of who you are can help you," Ananda continued, "but the truth is beyond your intellect and requires your own personal experience to verify. Honestly, Refugio, you can never know the truth of who you are from any concept I speak, because what you are hearing from me right now are simply words, which each have their own stories. To know if what I am saying is true, you must look within your own experience. If these words do not align with that, then by all means let them go."

Ananda sat down on a nearby branch of the silk rainbow tree that appeared to make a perfect seat for him. Wanting to continue this conversation, Refugio sat on the ground near his new acquaintance and began munching on his left over stuffed roll, which was just as delicious as he remembered it to be. He trusted Ananda and felt a connection to him, even though he had just met him. He wasn't sure if he trusted Ananda because he could also read minds, or if it was his joyful disposition that gave the impression of having everything and needing nothing. Refugio began to reflect on the other men he had met earlier on his trip. He remembered the things they had said to him and the stories they had told. Ananda looked out at the sky as if remembering some experience or person he once knew.

"Sometimes when people hear a story told by another storyteller, they give away their freedom and believe whatever that story is," Ananda noted. "People can exist in these stories for entire lifetimes. It can be difficult to let go of these stories because they are sometimes told to them by people that they respect and love. But really, it doesn't matter who it came from. All that matters is if you STILL believe the story."

Ananda smiled. "This is what you were just about to do when I approached you, Refugio. You believed what this man said about your life story and it could have haunted your entire existence, if you let it. To give away your power as a storyteller to one who does not see who you really are denies your personal freedom to create your own story. This can be, as you were just experiencing, very painful and sad."

Ananda looked down at Refugio with a sincere expression.

"It is important to understand, Refugio, that whatever another person's story about you is, it is only a reflection of who they think they are, and whatever story they are telling themselves. Do you remember what the men you recently met, thought of you?"

Refugio thought for a moment before replying "Well, the first man I met on my trip called me a 'nobody' just like he used to be. He thought that he was nothing without his power and wealth, and I guess he thought the same of me."

"Yes," replied Ananda. "This man thought his wealth is what gave him his significance. There is nothing wrong with being wealthy and having power and prestige, but when you believe that these things complete you, you will never know your intrinsic value. Refugio, you and everyone you meet are valuable and worthy of love simply because of who you are and not because of anything you do or have. Both of these men did not see who you really are. They created a limited and sad story about you because they were suffering deeply within themselves, from their own stories."

Refugio felt a sense of peace as Ananda's words fully seeped into his mind.

"How about the second man you met?" asked Ananda.

"Well," Refugio reflected, "The second man thought I had a very sad story and looked at me with pity. He thought being without a family made me pitiful."

Ananda nodded. "He could not see beyond the story he created for you because he could not see beyond his own. He was in a state called hopeless grief. To grieve the loss of a loved one is very natural and important. However, this man's grief was based upon hopelessness that is not consistent with reality. He believed that the love and connection he had with his family disappeared forever when their physical bodies were destroyed."

"Hopeless grief" Refugio thought to himself. He wondered why wouldn't all grief be hopeless?

Ananda, hearing Refugio's thoughts, smiled with assurance. "Don't worry Refugio, all of this will make more sense when you discover your forever story."

∞

"Guilt is based on a mistaken perception of life. Many people think that the root of their negative stories is fear, anger, or loss. Yet, the deeper root of all of these things is often guilt."

Chapter 10
Guilt

"Forever story?" Refugio thought to himself. Before he could ask he was reminded of something that confused Refugio when he met the grieving man. "I also heard something that the second man was saying to himself. It seemed to be the most miserable and dark part of his story. He just kept repeating to himself, I should of, I could of, I was a horrible father. Why was this man saying this and why did this feel like the most depressing part of his story?"

Ananda looked at Refugio sincerely, "This is the reason for most sad stories Refugio. This man was experiencing what is known as guilt."

"Guilt?" Contemplated Refugio. Ananda continued "Guilt is based on a mistaken perception of life. Many people think that the root of their negative stories is fear, anger, or loss. Yet, the deeper root of all of these things is often guilt. Everyone in this world will have mistakes and regrets. No one is perfect in their actions, words, or thoughts. Having a healthy remorse for one's actions can be productive to learning a better choice of action or thought. However, guilt is self-defeating and the cause of endless suffering. Remorse looks at your mistakes as lessons to

63

make better decisions that would lead to less suffering for oneself or others. Guilt however, looks at our mistakes as evidence that you are a bad person who is inherently evil and guilty. Guilt believes that our actions and unforgiveable. This is because guilt has no concept of eternity and thinks only within the realm of the temporary. There is endless suffering and guilt available to those who only believe in their temporary self. However, those who know who they really are will see that these mistakes and regrets are simply lessons in the greater reality of their forever story."

"The forever story? What is the forever story?"

Ananda smiled as he leaned forward, as if letting Refugio in on a profound, well-kept secret.

"Your forever story is your freedom," he said simply.

By then it had been dark for hours and the second moon was disappearing over the horizon, signaling half night. Refugio tried to maintain an alert, upright posture, but his drooping eyes gave away his oncoming sleepiness. Ananda smiled, a reassuring relaxed smile.

"We have had a long day together, Refugio," he said, "and I am glad you are so excited to learn. But let's take a rest tonight. Sleep well and I will show you what your forever story is tomorrow."

Though still eager to hear more, Refugio did not object. Ananda laid down under the beautiful silk rainbow tree. He seemed able to make a home wherever he happened to be. He rested his cane on a branch and his head on a mossy rock, then proceeded to fall asleep without effort.

The tree softly swayed in the night sky. The moon made the multicolored flowers of the rainbow silk tree appear to be glowing. Little light bugs swirled and danced around the branches like a midnight party. The lights of the stars were blending into the light bugs as Refugio's gaze became increasingly blurry with an oncoming sleepiness. He rested his head on his backpack and covered up with his blanket, still reflecting on the blissful man's words.

Refugio listened to the deep breathing of Ananda sleeping soundly as he contemplated the stories he had seen in people over the years. He wondered how many of these people were suffering because they were simply believing in a story that others had told them, or believing in a negative story they told themselves. He wondered what pain they might avoid and what kind of miraculous stories they could create, if they knew they were the storytellers. He thought about "the forever story" and wondered how that could explain what Ananda had said earlier about how he was connected to all things. The depressing story that was told to him earlier, by the sad man, seemed wonderfully distant, disappearing as easily as the stars when he closed his eyes. He slowly dozed off and slept deeper and more peacefully than he had in years.

∞

"Before Refugio could fall back into his old story and the painful emotions that followed, Ananda looked at Refugio and said, "You awake?!"

Chapter 11
Patterns of Thinking

Refugio awoke suddenly to a loud chuckle. Ananda was up and full of energy, as if he had been awake for hours. It was morning and Ananda seemed incredibly entertained as his head was swiveling swiftly, watching birds, until it stopped and focused on a mother bird that was feeding her baby. Refugio enjoyed the scene with Ananda, but suddenly a thought crept into his mind. He thought about how lucky this bird was who knew its mother and was receiving its care and comfort. He thought about how he never had a mother and how he missed out on this thing that was so important. Before Refugio could fall back into his old story and the painful emotions that followed, Ananda looked at Refugio and said, "You awake?!"

"Yes, sir, I slept very well and peacefully last night," Refugio replied, feeling a bit startled by Ananda's voice. "I did not expect to sleep like that on this trip."

"I'm sure that you will receive much that you do not expect in this life, but this will never change your forever story."

"Yes, the forever story," Refugio said to himself remembering where they left off the previous night.

∞

"Knowing your forever story makes any story in this life a blessed one, regardless of your temporary circumstance. It is the happy ending to all stories, thoughts, and dreams."

Chapter 12
The Forever Story

"Let's take a walk, Refugio."

Refugio got up and began to follow Ananda. He walked briskly and smoothly, his steps so soft it almost looked as if he floated while he moved. Refugio was surprised that this old man with a cane could move so quickly, and he had a hard time keeping up.

"I call it the forever story," Ananda began, "but it's really more than that, because all stories change and have a beginning and ending. But your forever story has no beginning and no ending. It is changeless, and it is who you really are."

"Unending? Forever? Who I really am?"

"Yes, Refugio, you heard right," Ananda chuckled. "Let me show you."

A few moments later, they arrived at a small stream. The water looked pure and lively as it passed along the rocks through the grassy landscape. Ananda crouched down and dipped his hands in the water. Refugio followed behind and did the same. Although he had seen and felt water many times before, for some reason he had the feeling as if he was experiencing it for the first time. He let the water pass through his hands, studying it intently.

"Let's look at the story of water, shall we?" Ananda said as Refugio stared at the stream. He noticed every splash and wave as it caressed through the rocks and dirt. Ananda began to speak as Refugio continued to be entranced by the water. "Do you realize that this is the same water that existed billions of years ago, and this water will exist billions of years from now?"

Refugio thought deeply about what Ananda said. He thought about all the things this water has done in this time, and the many different forms and places where it existed and will exist in the future. Refugio always loved the sound and feel of rushing water, but until this moment he had never felt such happiness and peace looking at this particular stream and feeling its current.

"You see, Refugio, every drop of this water will eventually vaporize. It then spends time in a cloud of purification and returns again as a droplet falling through the sky, ready for another ride. It does this simply for the joy of the journey."

Suddenly, a vision of a rain storm appeared within Refugio's mind, and he saw this process as Ananda spoke. Refugio saw a sky full of clouds and moisture that began to fall dramatically from the sky and caused gushing streams to form on the drenched ground. Then, suddenly, the vision of the storm was replaced by a large mountain with brilliant sheets of snow covering its surface. Snow was falling in every direction as Refugio watched the snowflakes merge into the white abyss of the snow banks.

"Water can also be frozen and become a unique snowflake that the world has never before seen, but when it melts it returns to its natural state ready to take on another journey," Ananda explained. "Even though this unique snowflake is fragile and short lived, it does not change its real identity as water. Water lives in eternity because it is never destroyed, only transformed. Do you know something else that can never be created or destroyed?"

"I'm not sure?" Questioned Refugio.

"Have you ever heard of the law of energy? Energy can also never be created or destroyed, and everything in the universe can be broken down into energy. What do you think you are made out of, Refugio?"

"Energy?" Responded Refugio inquisitively.

"That's right, my friend. Everything you see is made out of energy, including your body. Realize that because you are made out of energy, the real you can never be created or destroyed, only transformed. Your form will change, just like water, but the substance of your real nature will exist, forever. It always has and always will."

Refugio observed that Ananda was speaking with the excitement of a young child.

"That is why, just like water, you also live in eternity!" To emphasize his point, Ananda proceeded to splash Refugio with the water, playfully flashing a childlike grin. Refugio smiled and stood up, still taking in all that was just told to him.

"You said last night that my forever story would explain to me how we are all connected," he said to Ananda. "Are you saying because we are made out of the same thing we are connected to each other as well?"

"Good thinking, Refugio, you are catching on quick."

Again, Ananda splashed Refugio, only this time as the water hit Refugio's face, his eyes immediately closed and a new vision appeared of a beautiful ocean. In the vision, the sky above the ocean was colorful and full of stars and planets that Refugio had never before seen. In the ocean there were great waves that crashed and made the most beautiful scene. He felt as if he was actually on the beach watching the waves rise and fall again and again.

"Refugio, your life is like one of those waves. When the water rises out of the ocean, we call this a wave. A wave exists in time because it has an ending, and is temporary, just like our present physical form. When the wave crashes, you could consider this an ending or a death, but ultimately it is always the ocean. The distinctions of time, life, and death only happen when we define the wave as being separate from the ocean. The wave is very similar to how many people view their story in life—disconnected, separate, and temporary. This is of course a fictional story because ultimately, we are all connected just like the wave is to the ocean. It is also for this reason that you and I can read minds. Even though it seems like we are separate, we are made of the same substance and ultimately are the same thing."

Refugio's eyes had opened, and he began gazing into the stream as Ananda continued.

"If you remember you are not just a wave, but forever the ocean, you will see the stories of separation, loss, loneliness, and death are just stories that disappear into the vastness of the forever story. Knowing your forever story makes any story in this life a blessed one, regardless of your temporary circumstance. It is the happy ending to all stories, thoughts, and dreams. It is a positive outlook, in even the most depressing creations. It is seeing the tranquil horizon in the midst of a tragic storm. It is the positive and hope-filled thoughts that replace thoughts of grief and loss. It is the end of guilt and the end of the false perception that this present form of life is all there is. It is the eternal forgiveness in the mist of our greatest regrets and mistakes. Your forever story is the truth that sets you free. Your forever story IS your freedom."

Ananda stopped talking, and the vision completely disappeared.

They sat in silence listening to the stream and watching the colors the sun was creating on its surface. Refugio contemplated what Ananda had said. He was amazed by the visions that appeared, for he had never seen any place so beautiful before. He felt as if what the blissful man was saying made perfect sense logically, yet it was so different from the way he and everyone he had ever met had thought about life. He wondered how many other people knew that we were all connected and eternal. He wondered what kind of world he would live in if people understood these simple truths, and what kind of outlook it would give to stories of loss, grief, guilt and suffering.

After a deep breath, Ananda looked at Refugio, smiled, then stood up. Refugio proceeded to follow him.

They walked back together toward the silk rainbow tree, which Refugio could see in the distance. He noticed something different about the tree and nature that surrounded him. He could see that beyond the unique shapes and colors, they were made of the same substance. This substance made up everything, including his body. Refugio began to look at his hands with wonder, noting that the present form of his body was made up of the same substance that permeated the tree, the plants, and all of the life that surrounded him.

As they reached the tree, Refugio could feel the calmness and contentment that permeated the tree's being. He felt the breeze push the leaves, and he felt the joy that came from the rain that fell on its branches and nourished its roots. Taking a deep breath, Refugio was filled with the joy and love he felt in being connected to the life that surrounded him, in the presence of the forest. For most of Refugio's life he felt like he was alone but this was the first time Refugio stopped feeling lonely.

∞

"Happiness is what you truly are beyond your endless thinking. Happiness may not be the best word because people associate happiness with a happening. What you and everyone truly are is causeless happiness, happiness without a reason."

Chapter 13
Our Natural State

Ananda was watching Refugio as he pulled his hand away from the tree.

"How do you feel now, Refugio?" he asked with a smile.

"I can't even begin to explain it," Refugio replied. "I guess happiness is the best word I can use to define it, but it's way beyond that."

"Yes, words have their limits, but let's use happiness for now. There is something interesting about happiness that very few people know. Most believe that happiness must be achieved by doing something." Ananda paused to look at Refugio. "Happiness is actually your natural state."

"My natural state?" Refugio was puzzled. "I've got to think about that."

"That's funny you say that, because you actually think yourself out of 'that.' Happiness is what you truly are beyond your endless thinking. Happiness may not be the best word because people associate happiness with a happening. What you and everyone truly are is a causeless happiness, happiness without a reason."

"Happiness without reason…" said Refugio, his mind flooding with questions.

"Speaking of reasons, do you remember the reason you were going on this journey?" Ananda asked before Refugio could put words into any of those questions.

"Yes Ananda, I decided to walk all the way to the Dark Sea until I found out who I was. It seems so magnificent with its dark purple waves and black sand."

"The Dark Sea, eh? You're not that far away now," Ananda noted. "You could probably make it there in less than a day. I'm heading in that direction and can join you for part of your journey. If you would like the company, that is."

"I would love that! I am enjoying meeting you, and in a way, I almost feel like I have known you all my life."

"The feeling is mutual, my friend. In a way we have always known each other." And then Ananda chuckled.

Refugio pondered that possibility, but before he could say anything Ananda picked up his cane, canteen, and a small bag and began walking at a quick, smooth pace. Refugio scrambled to grab his things and catch up. They walked through trees, over streams, and through valleys. For a long time, they were silent, as Ananda's pace kept Refugio slightly out of breath, struggling to keep up. Ananda maintained a steady rhythm with each step and to Refugio's amazement the old man passed over obstacles without slowing even the slightest bit. A few hours later, much to Refugio's relief, Ananda stopped for a rest on a large rock on the summit of a hill. As Refugio sat down, he slowly took in the view of the upcoming landscape. The area they were entering was filled with crops of all kinds for as far as he could see. The surface of the hills was filled with the uniformity of the crops, giving the horizon an unreal beauty that looked more like a painting than real life.

∞

"Peace, happiness, and bliss is your REAL self, beyond all
of your thoughts, stories, and body."

Chapter 14
Deeper into The Natural State

Refugio and Ananda continued to absorb the beautiful scenery of the landscape around them in silence and peace. After a few moments, Refugio's mind circled back to what Ananda had said about the natural state. He was trying to think of a question to ask Ananda to explain it deeper, but once again Ananda spoke first.

"Have you ever seen a newborn child?"

Refugio smiled as he recalled a baby he once knew in the orphanage.

"Yes, I have," he replied.

"And what do you remember about this baby?"

"I remember a baby boy I used to know. He seemed to be peaceful, playful, and fascinated with life. He appeared to get joy from almost anything. That is, of course, until he started to cry."

"Yes, babies are naturally happy and joyous until they have some issue—they are hungry, soiled, or uncomfortable. When you take away its pains and discomforts, a baby is very peaceful and happy. This is not the case with most adults, even when they have all their basic comforts met. They will still have many fears, worries, and negative stories that distract them from this natural state of happiness. People are refreshed when they see a child because it is completely satisfied in itself. It is difficult for even the most depressed people not to feel joy when they hear a baby laugh. If everyone could remember their natural state from these infant teachers, this world would be full of blissful storytellers."

Refugio pondered that baby he once knew. He recalled the unforgettable giggling when Refugio would play peekaboo with him. He took a deep breath, absorbing the landscape surrounding them. Looking around, he noticed the crops dancing in the wind, which reminded him of the ocean in his vision. He then began to think about the Dark Sea and became inspired and energized to continue his journey.

Sensing Refugio's excitement, Ananda got up. They began walking together, but this time Refugio kept stride, filled with the anticipation of seeing the Dark Sea.

"Let's look deeper at your natural state," Ananda spoke as they walked. "Not only do you see this natural happiness in a baby, you also observe this when someone is in a state of deep sleep. When you are sleeping soundly, how would you feel if something unexpectedly woke you up?"

"I probably would be annoyed." Refugio replied.

"Sure you would. This is because it took you out of a state of peace. You see, when you are in deep sleep and without thoughts, stories, or any awareness of your body, you are completely happy and satisfied. Everyone wants a sound sleep at night and experiences much happiness when they do. This is also the reason people love drinking moon dust and become intoxicated with it. The intoxicant does not bring happiness, but the shutting down of thoughts that the intoxicant ensues is what allows you to temporarily experience your natural state. This is because peace, happiness, and bliss is your REAL self, beyond all of your thoughts, stories, and body."

Refugio thought about the experience he had drinking the rich man's moon dust. He remembered his first sip and how he felt a temporary peace when his thoughts seemed to slow down. He also remembered how the feeling didn't last very long and left him wanting more.

Ananda continued, "It is too bad that these people don't realize that they could experience this happiness without any intoxicant, just by remembering who they truly are. When you recognize this, you will realize that your natural state is your greatest gift in life!"

∞

"Your imagined self believes in death, but your real self knows eternity. Your imagined self believes in separation, loneliness and fear, but your real self knows connection, unending love and security. Your imagined self believes in guilt, regret and failures, yet your real self knows forgiveness, lessons and joy."

Chapter 15
Accepting Emotions

"I do feel very happy right now, but I do not feel happy all the time," Refugio admitted. "How could this be my natural state if I only experience this momentarily? I mean, I have many other emotions other than just happiness, and they change all the time."

"Yes, your thoughts and emotions do change all the time. In fact, it is their very nature to constantly change. However, these changing thoughts and emotions are not what you are. I am not saying that you will always experience happy thoughts, emotions, and experiences. I am saying that happiness IS experiencing these changing thoughts, emotions, and experiences. If you believe that you should experience happiness all the time, anytime you do not experience this happiness you would feel like a failure. This belief would be self-defeating and unrealistic. Remembering your natural state is about finding the happy, eternal, free, and detached observer in the midst of the variety of emotions life has to offer.

You have seen many people's thoughts and emotions throughout your life, and have observed many stories. Some were filled with pain and suffering and others were filled with joy and excitement. Having emotions ranging from despair to hope is very common. You don't need to reject these different emotions. It is actually by accepting them that you will be more able to let them go. Realize these emotions do come and go. However, identifying yourself with a thought pattern or emotional state, is just as illogical as identifying yourself with the clothes you put on today."

Refugio reflected on the minds of the many people he had watched throughout his life. He remembered seeing this vast range of emotions in different stories he heard."

"Remember too Refugio, that your thoughts and emotions will vary greatly, depending on how you are viewing your story. If you are viewing your story from your imagined self, your life will be subject to much suffering and your emotions will reflect that. If you remember your forever story, your thoughts and the corresponding emotions will be based in joy. It is all in what you think you "know" about life. Your imagined self believes in death, but your real self knows eternity. Your imagined self believes in separation, loneliness and fear, but your real self knows connection, unending love and security. Your imagined self believes in guilt, regret and failures, yet your real self knows forgiveness, lessons and joy. Every day we have the choice how we will view our story and we can change it at any moment."

Ananda went on. "People suffer so deeply in this life because they never challenge the things they believe against their inner knowledge. Along with this, they identify WITH their temporary thoughts and emotions. They believe they ARE their state of mind, and not the eternal causeless happiness that is observing whatever story the mind is currently producing. You can never be the impermanent or temporary, because you are that which is present before, during, and after any mental or emotional state."

∞

"When your body is eventually no longer useful, you will soon find out that your awareness continues existing. There is truly no such thing as death, only a dissolving of the physical shell most call themselves."

Chapter 16
Unchanging Blissful Awareness

Refugio thought about what Ananda had said about being present before and after any thought or story, and he nodded for Ananda to continue.

"Your emotional and mental states come and go with the seasons of life, but there is a blissful awareness that remains during all of these changes and seasons," Ananda explained.

"I'm not sure I understand," said Refugio, but that word "blissful" made Refugio think about how Ananda was truly a blissful being.

"Okay," Ananda said with a heart-warming laugh, "let me explain it another way. When was the last time you went to a movie?"

"Actually, I only went one time in my life but I'll never forget it. I saw an action movie. There were explosions, car chases, and an exciting story."

"Good, Refugio. You paid attention to the movie, but did you notice the screen that displayed all of these car chases and explosions?"

"I guess I never really thought about that."

"Yes, most people know their story and body very well, but they never give thought to the awareness that their body, thoughts, and emotions exist within. Your awareness is like the screen that the movie appears upon. There may be explosions and fire on the screen, but does the screen become burnt by the fire or damaged by an explosion?"

"No, of course not. The screen remains the same."

"Yes, Refugio, the screen remains unaffected by any of the scenes that are presented upon its surface. If the movie has water, the screen does not get wet. If the screen is covered in fire, it is not burned. This is because the screen is the surface that all these experiences are projected upon. Similarly, your natural state is the blissful awareness that all life is projected upon. This always remains the same regardless of what is being projected upon it, or even the absence thereof. These projections include your body, relationships, stories, experiences, thoughts, and emotions. Just look for yourself, at your own situation, to see if what I am saying is true."

Refugio wondered exactly what Ananda meant by looking at his own situation, and the blissful man naturally became aware of the young man's confusion.

"My friend, you had an idea about who you were when I met you, and now you have a different idea, but the 'you' that was aware of these ideas remains. If you develop a new story about yourself, the awareness of this new story will be the same awareness of your old story. These stories and their corresponding emotions and thoughts are always changing, but the natural you is changeless. It is not only these stories that are changing all the time; your body is constantly going through transformations as well."

Refugio looked down at his body, thinking about its transformational nature, as he continued walking.

"You once had a child's body, now you have a man's body, and someday you will have an older body like myself," said Ananda. "But the real you who is aware of this body is the same awareness that has always been."

"Always been? Like forever Always?" asked Refugio.

"Yes," laughed Ananda. "You have this awareness when you are without your body's senses in sleep, and you will also have it when you eventually leave your present physical body in the process known as 'death.' This is, of course, just death of the physical shell that your awareness was temporarily attached to. When you were sleeping and had no use of your physical senses, you were still conscious, aware, and creating. Your awareness and ability to create continues without the use of your physical senses during sleep. This process of creating, existing, and perceiving is not hindered by the disuse of the physical body. Realize that when your body is eventually no longer useful, you will soon find out that your awareness continues existing. There is truly no such thing as death, only a dissolving of the physical shell most call 'themselves.'"

"That makes sense but only to a point," replied Refugio. "If it is true that awareness is deathless, then how come I don't remember being aware of anything before this life?"

"Good question, Refugio. Just like everything else, we can see the answer by looking at our life experience. Forgetfulness does not equate to non-existence. You do not remember what it was like being an infant, but this does not mean your infancy was non-existent. You also have forgotten many dreams in your sleep but your awareness was still very much functioning during these dream adventures."

Refugio remembered his dream from the beginning of his journey.

Ananda continued, "Have you ever heard people say they don't 'feel old' even though their body is aged, and they have been through many different experiences?"

"Yes, I have," said Refugio. "I have also felt this way myself. I mean, I think differently than I did as a child, but there is a part of me that seemed like it was always the same, kind of like it is ageless."

"Ageless is right," Ananda agreed. "Even though everything around us is changing and aging, our awareness is eternal, and eternity is timeless. It is this awareness, which is your natural self, that is the eternal, changeless, and causeless happiness. This eternal happiness is what everyone searches for in this world of shift and change, but it is only those who look to their real self that will find the changeless happiness to be their natural identity. All beings in this world search for happiness, but it is only a few who realize happiness is what they truly are."

Ananda jumped over a small stream, and Refugio followed. A group of birds flew out of a tree just ahead of them as they created a rustling noise while stepping through an area of heavy brush. Ananda was again leading the way, carefully pushing branches out of their path.

∞

"This is why we play games in the first place, for our enjoyment. Even though you may lose in the game, you know that after the game is finished you remain the same, unaffected by the outcome and free to play another."

Chapter 17
Life, The Joyful Game

Refugio was inspired and curious as he thought about what Ananda had said while navigating through the brush.

"Ananda, how would a person who knew their natural identity view the world?" he asked a few minutes later.

Ananda was watching the birds fly away with an entertained smile.

"Good question," he said, turning his attention back to Refugio. "It is difficult to make any hard and fast rules of one who remembers their real self, because every storyteller is unique. Nevertheless, maybe this example will help. If you were playing a game, like a board game or video game, and temporarily forgot you were just playing, you might become fully identified with your player and become miserable when your player is in a bad situation. When you remember that you are just playing a game, however, you may again enjoy the process of playing, regardless of your temporary position. This is why we play games in the first place, for our enjoyment. Even though you may lose in the game, you know that after the game is finished you remain the same, unaffected by the outcome and free to play another. The one who knows who they are sees life like a joyful game. They see the temporary for what it is and know they themselves are the eternal. They enjoy every moment and whatever situation they are experiencing without forgetting who they truly are. Remember this Refugio, the majority of mental struggles stem from taking this life too seriously and forgetting this joyful game of life."

"But Ananda, questioned Refugio, if people don't take life seriously wouldn't they just hurt each other?"

"Actually Refugio, it is because people take life too seriously that they end up hurting each other. You are truly freed up to love others, when you are not taking life so seriously. Does a father take time to play with his children when he is stressed about his career? Does a young man smile at passing strangers when he is worried about his future? Does a woman forgive and love others when she is dwelling in guilt over her past?"

"When one knows at the end of this experience they return to their state of eternity and happiness, they are free to enjoy this gift of life. It is much easier to be peaceful when you know you are always safe. Easier to love others when you yourself know you are loved. Easier to forgive when you know you are forgiven. Easier to give when you know that you are in need of nothing. Looking at life as a joyful game does not mean one lives carelessly or recklessly. It also does not hinder one from living skillfully, to the best of their ability. On the contrary, viewing life this way actually helps one make the best possible decisions, without letting a disturbed or fearful mind make rash choices that could cause unnecessary pain to themselves or others."

"I guess I understand what you mean," Refugio acknowledged, "but how can I know that I remain the same regardless of my situation in life? I mean, I still really feel like I am this body and mind, and I have a hard time just letting go. I want to believe that I will always be okay, and that the real me is eternal, but I just don't know."

Refugio had never been a person to believe something without experiencing it for himself. He was naturally inquisitive, but not gullible.

They entered a large field, leaving the brush behind. The land flattened out, making their steps increasingly seamless and effortless.

"Refugio, I don't want you to believe anything," Ananda said soothingly. "My words cannot be the truth because the truth is beyond words. Every word has its own story and meaning, depending on the storyteller's interpretation. These words can point you to an experience of truth, but experience will be needed for you to personally validate it. As I said earlier, you can hear the recipe of an apple pie, but you must taste the pie yourself."

"For one to truly understand they must deeply inquire into their own mind and self. There is nothing that one must do to 'earn' who they are, but without deep self-inquiry this gift will remain covered. This is similar to trying to look out a window to see a beautiful view, but the window was covered in dirt. Spending quality time cleaning the window would help you tremendously to see this view more clearly. There are many effective methods for cleaning this 'window,' and simply hearing and contemplating my words is one of them. Remember though, cleaning the window did not create the beautiful view that was already there."

∞

"These emotions and thoughts left Refugio unaffected in any way, as he continued feeling the bliss permeating his own being. The feeling of peace and happiness was perpetual, as he was simply aware, and not attached to the ever-changing thoughts and emotions."

Chapter 18
Out of Body

Ananda stopped walking and looked intently at Refugio, pondering whether or not to do or say something. Refugio stopped walking and looked curiously at Ananda.

"Okay, my friend, let me show you," Ananda said with a quick smile. With his free hand he gently tapped Refugio on his forehead lightly, and as the words "show you" left Ananda's mouth, Refugio suddenly became overcome with a strange feeling of dizziness. His vision became blurry and the trees and plants that surrounded him began spinning. Faster and faster they traveled, and Refugio started to become frightened. In a panic, he cried out. "Ananda!"

Suddenly, to Refugio's surprise, he was no longer standing but floating above the ground, near the tops of the surrounding trees. The feeling of dizziness was gone, along with the panic, replaced by an incredible peace. Looking around, he had the strange and comforting sensation of being safe and somehow home. A bliss he had never experienced before was permeating his entire being. It reminded him of the tranquility he experienced when he was just about to fall asleep, although in this state he was totally conscious and intensely aware.

Refugio now became aware of a small figure below him, and he began to try to focus on who this figure was. It looked familiar in some way, but he couldn't put his finger on it. He studied the body for a while and suddenly, to his astonishment, he realized it was his own body! He was looking at himself, or at least what he thought was himself, which was now 15 feet below him. Next to his own body was the body of Ananda. They both sat motionless. Refugio was trying to process how he could be above and apart from his body and yet still very much existing and aware.

His attention was then diverted from his body to the surrounding atmosphere. The limited point of view he was used to evaporated into an increased awareness that encompassed all the surrounding life. He felt the vastness of his own presence; it seemed as if there were no borders to his being. All around him he could see life in many different forms coming into physical existence and dying off. He was aware of the planets spinning and the moons and stars that surrounded the world traveling in their own orbit. There was the experience of life happening in all directions, but he was pleasantly unaffected by all of it.

"Welcome to your real self."

Refugio sensed Ananda speaking, but there was no vocal sound. The words traveled through the atmosphere as thoughts, without the need of sound. And yet, these thoughts were clearer than any words he had heard in his whole life. "My real self," Refugio replied with his thoughts, which echoed in his mind, bouncing through the atmosphere of Refugio's awareness. Ananda again spoke with his mind. "Look to see the thoughts surrounding you." Refugio became instantly aware that he was encircled by countless thoughts. Thoughts about himself, thoughts about his life, desires, goals, and motives. He could also hear thoughts of millions of people. Their lives, stories, plans, worries, and fears. They traveled like waves in and out of his awareness, creating and leaving behind clouds of emotions. Some were full of joy, others full of sadness. Coming and going like waves, they danced upon his consciousness. These emotions and thoughts left Refugio unaffected in any way, as he continued feeling the bliss permeating his own being. The feeling of peace and happiness was perpetual, as he was simply aware, and not attached to the ever-changing thoughts and emotions.

For a moment, everything Ananda had been saying made perfect sense. Refugio was now the blissful awareness beyond his body, thoughts, and emotions. He knew there was no real death because he was something beyond the physical body. All fears disappeared and a feeling of love surrounded Refugio, and it began increasing with his awareness. Like an exploding star, Refugio's presence seemed to expand in all directions. The world disappeared, and only this deep feeling of love remained. To Refugio, this love was the only thing that was real, as the world now evaporated like a dream when awakening. All around him was love and out of this unending love, a single conscious thought bubbled into existence. "My real self."

Suddenly, the dizziness returned and he again began to feel the constructs of his own physical body. The heaviness of this frame seemed unnatural and foreign to him. His awareness and vision was again restricted by his eyeballs, and he felt the borders of his body and senses. He took a gasp of air as if restarting his body's functions. As he took several deep breaths, he was again becoming accustomed to his body while at the same time attempting to contemplate his experience. Refugio looked at his figure and put his hands on his chest as if to make sure it was real. As he continued trying to become established in his physical existence, he heard Ananda's voice.

"Refugio, how did you like your real Self?"

There was a long pause as Refugio had trouble using his voice to speak. Ananda was chuckling, for he understood that Refugio would have a difficult time putting his experience into words and that he was still trying to adapt to himself.

"That was amazing!" Refugio was finally able to say. Ananda broke out in a laugh, which encouraged Refugio to continue expounding on his experience. "I felt so alive and awake! That experience of the world seemed like it was more real than this one is here. I felt the experience of being everlasting bliss, regardless of the changing thoughts and emotions and bodies that surrounded me." Ananda's smile lit up his eyes.

There was a long pause, as Refugio and Ananda sat in a blissful silence. Refugio felt very close to Ananda as he now understood how this blissful man was experiencing life. The wind softly blew the surrounding plants. The scene appeared to be casual, which seemed to contradict the amazing and exciting experience that had just occurred.

"I'm not sure what that was, but that was the first time in my life that I felt like I was home, safe, and truly happy. It felt like that is what I had been searching for all along," Refugio said softly.

"Yes, Refugio, home is wherever you are. The treasure was so close you overlooked its presence within you. You were like a flower trying to find beauty, or a star trying to find light. Searching for greatness in the world, you didn't see the greatness in yourself."

Refugio smiled in contentment of his new realization, but before he could settle his mind Ananda spoke.

"Speaking of greatness, did you see what is past the hills?" asked Ananda, pointing to the horizon with his cane.

∞

"He felt fearless as he enjoyed his physical body but knew that he was something greater than this temporary shell."

Chapter 19
Almost There

Refugio was so overcome by his experience that he had not noticed that on the horizon was a sliver of the Dark Sea. He could now see the faint shadow of its black waves and endless waters on the skyline. With the excitement of reaching the Dark Sea quickly altering his focus, he jumped up on a rock to get a better view. This was the first time he had even seen a large body of water, and such a unique sight. It looked endless and its dark horizon seemed as if it went on forever. Refugio looked over at Ananda and was pleased to see the same excitement reflected back to him.

"Well, what are we waiting for?" asked Ananda, with a familiar laugh. "Let's go for it!"

As Ananda got up and took off, Refugio hustled to follow his companion. They bolted ahead with the exuberance of two young children, as they headed right for the water. They moved smoothly and quickly, as Ananda skillfully maneuvered obstacles and Refugio followed close behind.

Refugio was more alive than ever. As he hopped and skipped over rocks and branches, he felt what an amazing creation his body was. He felt fearless as he enjoyed his physical body but knew that he was something greater than this temporary shell. A deep sense of happiness and contentment dawned in Refugio's mind as he danced through the landscape. When Ananda slowed down, Refugio reduced his pace as well.

∞

"There is nothing wrong with wanting to be more, for it is the expression of life that causes us to want to be more. However, when people think that by becoming more they will no longer be nothing, they pursue this more out of a false sense of lack."

Chapter 20
The Funny Thing about Happiness

"Good, Refugio, you have almost achieved your goal of reaching the Dark Sea. Are you as happy as you thought you'd be when you arrived?"

Refugio thought for a moment. "I am happy, but not exactly because I am here," he replied. "I guess I am happier thinking about who I really am."

"Yes, Refugio, your goal was always this happiness. That's the funny thing about happiness—many think they will achieve happiness by doing something in the world. Assuming that happiness is within the objects, or experiences of the world, most never realize that happiness has always been within themselves. They are always desperately searching for more, never resting in the contentment of their real self."

Ananda jumped over a ditch and Refugio followed. "Yes, I think this is true," agreed Refugio. "Many people I have met seemed to have a feeling within themselves that they could achieve this happiness by doing more. More, more, more. I saw this clearly with the first man I met earlier on my journey, and many others I have met in my life. I even saw this in myself when I started this journey. I felt like if I could find my own story, one of greatness, then I would be more, and I thought this more would make me happy."

"Yes, this 'more' is the mantra of this and many other worlds you have not yet seen," Ananda explained. "There is nothing wrong with wanting to be more, for it is the expression of life that causes us to want to be more. However, when people think that by becoming more they will no longer be nothing, they pursue this more out of a false sense of lack. This is what reinforces a feeling of disconnection within. This imagined disconnection from love and happiness is the cause of so much suffering, both within individual minds and externally in the world. Try to realize, my friend, that people recklessly pursue this 'more' not because they are greedy, evil, or selfish. The root of this sense of lack has always been, and will always be, a need for unlimited unconditional love."

∞

"In your world, many people view relationships as the source that will provide them unconditional love. This causes much suffering and many problems, because another person cannot give you something that you already possess."

Chapter 21
The Need for Love

"Love," thought Refugio. He looked up, and the Dark Sea became closer in his vision. He could now take in the white foam from the crashing waves. The sun glittered on its surface, and the vastness seemed never ending. They slowed their pace even more as they came closer to the shore.

"Everyone in this universe has a deep need for unlimited happiness and love," Ananda began. Refugio thought that the blissful man's revelations were expanding along with the glorious view. "Notice, I did not say a want, I said a need. A want you can live without, but a need you will suffer greatly in its absence. There is no real absence of unlimited love, because you and everyone you will ever meet is unconditionally loved by all of life and the Creator of all life. It is only the perception and belief in the separation from this love, that causes the experience within your own mind. Realize, my friend, you and everyone else in the world are loved not because of anything you do, or do not do, but simply because of who you really are. Nothing can change this and nothing ever will. You cannot be any more loved than you truly always are, and this will NEVER change regardless of what relationships or situations come and go in your life."

Refugio considered the relationships he had growing up in the orphanage. He thought about how much he loved and missed his fellow orphan brothers and sisters already, in just the few days he had been gone.

Sensing Refugio's thoughts about his old friends, Ananda gently patted Refugio on the back.

"Relationships are a great place to see this need for love," he said. "In your world, many people view relationships as the source that will provide them unconditional love. This causes much suffering and many problems, because another person cannot give you something that you already possess. Remember this next point I tell you, Refugio, because someday you may meet a young lady and fall in love. And maybe someday is sooner than you think." Ananda laughed, and Refugio wondered what he meant by that last statement.

"It is those who see relationships as an opportunity to share the love they have within, rather than trying to depend on the love from another person, who will never experience a lack of love in their lives," Ananda continued. "Those who share their unlimited love with others freely will find it effortlessly within themselves."

Ananda and Refugio stopped as they finally arrived at the beach. The sound of the crashing waves was overwhelmingly pleasant and new to Refugio. Noticing how the waves would repeatedly build and then settle, he was reminded of the forever story. He knew that the waves would crash, only to return to the ocean again. He felt a deep peace in his heart, understanding how everything in nature followed this pattern. The trees, birds, plants, and animals all returned to their source, the planet, when they died. The truth was all around him and in everything he saw. The forever story was in all of life.

The smell of salt water was stronger than ever. A slight breeze blew off the surface, reflecting the sun in a sparkling dance that looked like an ocean of diamonds. Refugio was so overwhelmed by the ocean he didn't notice a tree a few feet in front of him. When Ananda pointed his cane toward the tree, Refugio followed him. They sat down at its base.

The tree was a purple raindrop tree, something Refugio had never seen before in real life because they were only found on coastlines. It had purple and red leaves that pointed directly at the ground, giving the tree an appearance of falling rain drops. He seemed to remember seeing this tree somewhere recently, then suddenly realized it was one of the trees on Ananda's cane! He looked at the cane and saw the many trees they had visited on this journey. There was the silk rainbow tree with its beautiful flowers, the blue wish tree he had dreamt under, the dead tree he fell against during his sad story, and there was the purple raindrop tree they sat under now. Refugio was astonished.

Noticing Refugio's realization Ananda spoke. "Yes, Refugio, this is all going according to plan. It is the plan of every creature to eventually awaken to who they always have been."

Refugio was too overcome with this realization to speak. He felt as if everything in life was working together to help him find himself. He felt as if there was a powerful, intelligent presence that was guiding his entire life. Ananda, the men he met on his journey, the trees, the nature that surrounded him—all of life seemed to respond in his quest. Refugio took a deep breath filled with the smell of salt, and he could feel the vibration of the crashing waters. He put his hands in the black sand. It felt warm and soft as he caressed its surface.

As Refugio was basking in the beautiful scene, Ananda opened a small bag he had been carrying and offered a blue star apple to Refugio. He gladly accepted the fruit, and they relaxed and ate. As he ate, Refugio began to deeply ponder his real nature as unending happiness, and also the world in which he lived. He felt as if he understood that his true self was eternal and unending happiness, but after a long timeless pause a question arose that almost startled him and broke his peace.

"Why is there a world, if ultimately all happiness and love dwells within?" he asked Ananda.

∞

"It is for the purpose of expressed happiness and love that this world exists. This life is a great adventure in which the eternal enjoys the temporary. It is where the changeless appreciate change. It is where the unified can love duality. It is where the perfect understand and accept imperfection. It is where the limitless overcome and value limitation."

Chapter 22
Purpose Creator and Creation

Ananda had heard Refugio's question, reading his thoughts.

"Now I'm going to explain something that is going to challenge everything I have been saying about happiness," he told Refugio. "What if I told you that this world is made FOR your happiness?" Ananda chuckled and leaned back into the tree.

Thinking out loud, Refugio replied, "For happiness? How is that possible? You just told me that happiness is within myself and there is no need to seek it in the world."

"I did indeed. Quite a paradox, isn't it? Nevertheless, Refugio, a paradox doesn't mean it is unexplainable. Like you have just realized, many people struggle deeply in this world trying to attain happiness that already exists within themselves. These people suffer greatly from their BELIEVED separation from their deepest needs and desires. What you think you need in your stories is endless. What your real self-possesses is infinite. When a person finds this unlimited happiness and love dwelling within, they will find the world a perfect place to express this happiness and love in any way they desire."

Ananda paused for a moment, allowing Refugio to keep up, before he resumed his lesson.

"It is for the purpose of expressed happiness and love that this world exists. This life is a great adventure in which the eternal enjoys the temporary. It is where the changeless appreciate change. It is where the unified can love duality. It is where the perfect understand and accept imperfection. It is where the limitless overcome and value limitation. Realize, my friend, that the creator of this world, your body, and the entire universe did this for your joy. At every moment you are given everything you need to experience the joy of your life. Every moment of this life is a gift of joy."

∞

"Everything that you believe you need, Refugio, is not necessarily everything your story requires. In fact, if you had gotten everything you think you needed, you would have never been able to express the amazing love you really are."

Chapter 23
The Final Revelation

With a baffled expression and gnawing doubt, Refugio responded, "Everything I need? I mean, really? I still sort of feel like I could've used a little more in my life, like a family, or a home. Everything you have shown me so far has been amazing, and I don't mean to sound ungrateful, but remember, I still never had a family. If this creation is for my joy, then why didn't the creator put a family in my life for me to enjoy?"

The suffering started to trickle back into Refugio's mind but Ananda cooled it instantly by putting his hand on Refugio's back looking at Refugio with an incredible sincerity and compassion.

"Everything you believe you need, Refugio, is not necessarily everything your story requires. In fact, if you had gotten everything you think you needed, you would have never been able to express the amazing love you really are."

The waves, the clouds and the wind that surrounded them all seemed to stop in pure silence, as if respecting the importance of Ananda's words.

"When you lived in the orphanage you were like a father to the young children. You became a brother to your peers. You were a compassionate heart to those who were lonely and scared. You were an encourager to those who were discouraged. You were a hope for those who felt hopeless. Refugio, you ARE the family you always sought in this life."

These words hit Refugio like a wave crashing down on the rocks of the nearby shore. He began to cry, and then he looked at Ananda and saw a fantastic light shining through his eyes. The light started small but soon expanded in intensity. Refugio could feel energy rushing across his skin as the light grew stronger and continued growing. The hairs on his arm were standing on end, and the energy gathered in his heart. He could feel a weight lifted off his chest as love radiated from his entire being.

Refugio now could no longer see Ananda or the world that surrounded Him. His entire vision, body, and senses were experiencing more and more of this loving light and energy that had come through Ananda's eyes. Within Refugio's awareness, flashes of pictures, concepts, and beliefs cascaded. Visions rushed through his mind with a quickness and a fury. Memories flooded in of the people in his life and the impact he had had on them. He was filled with a sense of pride and confidence, remembering his part in these young friends' lives. He struggled to keep his tears under control as he experienced a deep feeling of unconditional love that came from within.

He saw the perfection of his story and who he was vividly displayed, as if he were watching a movie in high speed. He saw himself growing up in the orphanage. He felt deeply how he had been a father, a brother, and a friend. He thought about how he was the only family that his orphan siblings had ever known. He saw the children whose lives he had helped change. He saw his journey to the Dark Sea, and the people he met along the way. He saw the rich man, and the sad man. He saw what they believed about life and reality. He saw everything he once thought of as a mistake but was now seen in its perfection. Every perceived loss was now recognized as fortune. Every fault was now understood as a virtue. He could see that every wrong turn had been another step towards his destiny. Everything in his life had a meaning—being an orphan, feeling alone, reading minds, meeting Ananda. The story he once despised and grieved was now perfection, and it was the only story that could help him wake up to who he was. Refugio knew now, without a doubt, that he was the storyteller, he was free, and his life was perfect.

∞

"He now traveled calmly without any urgency or resolve to complete any task. He felt for the first time that he was free to create whatever he wanted to create. His thoughts and desires came from a place of satisfaction."

Chapter 24
Life After Awakening

"Refugio, Refugio." The words could only be heard faintly. At last, Refugio opened his eyes. Slowly the light began to dissipate and he began to see the world again. It was the same scenery as before but it looked less solid and appeared to be permeating with the same love and light that came from Ananda's eyes. Refugio looked around, but Ananda and his things were gone. He searched everywhere trying to find his friend until he heard Ananda's laugh, which seemed to be coming from all directions.

"Ananda, where are you?"

"Don't worry, my friend," the voice replied. "I have not gone anywhere. I have more to show you in the future, when you are ready. There are worlds that you have never seen before and many more realities and dimensions than you can imagine. I am everywhere, as I have always been and will always be."

Refugio was overcome with the feeling of Ananda's presence even though he was not visible. He felt as if he were closer to Ananda than he had been throughout their entire journey. He experienced a deep sense of connection to his friend, giving him a comfort within his core even though he was now alone on the beach.

"You were wise, Refugio," the voice spoke again, "because you wished to find out who you truly are. You now know with absolute certainty that you are love and happiness, and that your story is one of perfection. You are free to express the unlimited love that you are, in any way that your blissful heart desires. Now my friend, all of your stories will be an expression of unlimited love. With this love write your story as an expression of your unlimited happiness. Write your story, Refugio, write your story."

The light and energy began to dissipate slowly as the voice faded. Ananda's last words seemed to ring out in Refugio's mind, leaving him thankful happy and free.

Refugio was overwhelmed with so much bliss he did not move for hours. He just sat in the sand and stared off into the seemingly endless horizon. The waves crashed and every sound and bubble generated by the water was like a piece of art that was being created simply for Refugio's delight. He enjoyed the breeze, the water, and himself. Eventually, he gathered his things, and again began walking. He now traveled calmly without any urgency or resolve to complete any task. He felt for the first time that he was free to create whatever he wanted to create. His thoughts and desires came from a place of satisfaction.

∞

"Refugio picked up the cane, smiled at Sita, grabbed her hand, and said with joy, "Would you like to know another story?""

Chapter 25
The New Teacher

For many days Refugio traveled aimlessly and happily, feeling the unconditional love that he was. He relished nature, and looking at the stars, and thinking about the worlds that Ananda would someday show him. He greeted everyone he met warmly, and he observed many stories, but behind all of them Refugio saw the forever story. Many did not know what to think of this wandering, happy young man, but Refugio did not care what others were thinking, because he was now living in his own heaven.

On his fifth day of wandering up the coastline, Refugio approached a large farm that overlooked the Dark Sea. He was enjoying his thoughts and admiring the crops when there approached a lady riding on a rundown tractor. She had short dark hair, a small frame, and brown eyes that to Refugio seemed to show a deep sadness. Refugio noticed that this woman was lifting huge bundles of sugarcane, which were larger than her, onto a tractor. She looked strained and tired as she continued to work in this exhausted manner. When the woman spotted Refugio, she was startled but quickly put on a fake smile, stopped working, walked over to Refugio, and introduced herself.

"My name is Sita (SEE-Ta) Can I help you?" she said.

"My name is Refugio. I was just admiring your sugarcane fields and enjoying this beautiful day."

"I guess it is a nice day, isn't it?" replied Sita. As she looked around for the first time during her busy day, she noticed the blue skies, and the sun sparkling off the sea.

"You look like you could use some help. Could I give you a hand?" Refugio asked.

"Oh, that would be a Godsend," she said with a sigh of relief. "I have been trying to get this done all day and I still have to get dinner ready for the kids."

"Well, okay then," said Refugio. "I can follow you alongside the tractor and throw the bundles in the back while you drive."

She thankfully agreed, and they worked together, finishing a job that alone would have taken Sita three hours in less than 45 minutes. Sita was amazed at the progress she made and grateful to Refugio for his help. She was normally shy when meeting new people, but to her Refugio seemed to have an attitude that expressed having everything and needing nothing. This quality gave her an almost instant trust in Refugio. Intuitively Refugio gave her a deep sense of peace.

After finishing with the sugarcane, Refugio was again staring at the Dark Sea with a child's look of wonder and enthusiasm. She watched his gaze for a few moments.

"You look like you could use some food. How about I pay you back for your work with a homemade dinner?" she asked.

Refugio looked at Sita, who was now standing at the coastline, and he noticed how her dark eyes matched the water, as if they were a part of the ocean.

"Yes, thank you, I would be grateful," he said with a smile. She smiled back, then turned off the tractor and began walking toward a large, quaint farmhouse that looked as if it were in need of slight repair. Refugio could see children playing in the yard. They swiftly ran into the house and disappeared when Sita called them to wash up for dinner.

When the two of them walked inside, Sita showed Refugio where he could clean up. As he looked around the rooms, he noticed a picture of a young man with Sita. She was holding a baby. Below the picture were a few items that looked as if they belonged to the man in the picture: a hat that looked similar to the one the man had in the picture, a ring, and a cane. The cane reminded Refugio of his teacher, the blissful man, and as he walked toward the washroom he smiled to himself.

As Refugio slowly began to clean up, he thought about the items and the picture. He realized that this was Sita's husband who had passed. He could hear the stomping of children and laughing above him. A few minutes later, he walked out into the dining room to find a freshly prepared meal, with two children sitting at the table. As Sita noticed Refugio's presence, she said with a smile and a glimmer in her eyes, "Thank you for joining us."

Refugio sat down at the table with the children who were gigging shyly at each other over their excitement for their new guest. The younger child looked at Refugio and asked timidly, "Do you play hide and seek?"

"I am a hide and seek master!" Refugio declared.

The children looked at each other with wide eyes, and the younger one asked, "Can you play with us after dinner?"

"Yes, but be prepared, I am very good," he said. Both children began to laugh, and their eyes lit up in anticipation of playing with Refugio.

As the children were laughing, Sita walked in with a platter with food that seemed enough to feed ten people.

As Refugio glanced, he noticed stuffed rolls, purple potatoes, blue star apples, and a multicolored salad with various vegetables. He could tell that Sita had gone above and beyond for this dinner, and he knew that he was not going to leave the table hungry. Refugio enjoyed the delicious dinner, and the playful banter with the children. There was even a split second were Refugio felt what it would be like to be part of this family. It felt good.

After they had finished eating, the children begged Refugio to play with them.

"I will join you in a few minutes, after I finish helping your mom clean up," he said.

Refugio began bringing dishes to the kitchen when he noticed Sita was lost in thoughts of her husband who had passed a few years prior. He could see how she acted happy around the children to hide her loss, but she was still suffering deeply in her own memories and emotions. To Refugio, there seemed to be a dark cloud that surrounded Sita and he could see how this affected everything she saw and experienced.

As they finished cleaning the dishes, she asked him if he would like to have a cup of tea. He agreed and they sat at the table. As she poured the tea Refugio began the conversation.

"Atman was the name of your husband you lost," he said confidently.

Sita looked shocked. "How did you know that, Refugio?" she asked.

Refugio looked at her with gentle sincerity and said, "I see what is hidden in people's thoughts. I can see what others think and feel. I have been like this ever since I was a child."

Although surprised, Sita responded with a brief pause that gave the impression of understanding.

"I know exactly what you mean, Refugio, because I used to have this same ability," she said. Noticing Refugio's surprise, she added, "I used to be able to see what others were thinking and feeling, but after my husband died I lost it all. I lost him, I lost the ability, and I lost my love for life. Everywhere I look now, I see only sorrow. If you can see my thoughts, Refugio, you must know I am a very sad person with a very sad story."

Refugio stared into her eyes with empathy and compassion, which gave Sita a feeling that someone truly understood her pain. Tears began falling from her eyes. She felt a release of grief that she had been hiding from her children for years. Refugio continued to look at her with great compassion as he recalled his own story, which had been full of pain, and he was reminded of the blissful man who helped him through it.

As Refugio was thinking of Ananda, the cane resting under the picture fell, creating a loud noise. It rolled right to Refugio's feet. The sound shook both Refugio and Sita. In Refugio's mind, he heard a soft chuckle and knew immediately that it was Ananda. A feeling of peace, calm, and bliss permeated the room, overcoming both of them. Sita looked around, trying to find the cause for her sudden change of feelings and the peace that she was experiencing.

Refugio picked up the cane, smiled at Sita, grabbed her hand, and said with joy, "Would you like to know another story?"

∞

The Storyteller

Made in the USA
San Bernardino, CA
12 December 2018